CARTER G. WOODSON

—African-American Biographies—

CARTER G. WOODSON

Father of African-American History

Series Consultant:
Dr. Russell L. Adams, Chairman
Department of Afro-American Studies, Howard University

Robert F. Durden

Enslow Publishers, Inc.

40 Industrial Road	PO Box 38
Box 398	Aldershot
Berkeley Heights, NJ 07922	Hants GU12 6BP
USA	UK

http://www.enslow.com

Library of Congress Cataloging-in-Publication Data

Durden, Robert Franklin.
    Carter G. Woodson : father of African-American history / Robert F. Durden.
       p. cm. — (African-American biographies)
    Includes bibliographical references and index.
    Summary: A biography of the son of former slaves who received a Ph.D. in
history from Harvard and devoted his life to bringing the achievements of his
race to the world's attention.
    ISBN 0-89490-946-0
    1. Woodson, Carter Godwin, 1875–1950—Juvenile literature.
2. Historians—United States—Biography—Juvenile literature.
3. Afro-American historians—Biography—Juvenile literature. 4. Afro-
Americans—Historiography—Juvenile literature. [1. Woodson, Carter Godwin,
1875–1950. 2. Educators. 3. Historians. 4. Afro-Americans—Biography.]
I. Title. II. Series.
E175.5.W65D87 1998
973'.0496073'007202
[B]—DC21   97-30243
                                             CIP
                                             AC
Printed in the United States of America

10 9 8 7 6 5

Illustration Credits: Courtesy of Archives and Special Collections, Robert W.
Woodruff Library, Atlanta University Center, Inc., p. 90; Berea College
Archives/Berea, KY, p. 31; Chicago Historical Society, p. 49; Courtesy of John
Hope Franklin, p. 112; Courtesy of The Crisis Publishing Co., Inc., the mag-
azine of the National Association for the Advancement of Colored People, pp.
55, 74; Courtesy of the United States Postal Service, p. 109; Fisk University
Library Archives, p. 78; Harvard University Archives, p. 41; Library of
Congress, pp. 34, 63, 94; National Archives, p. 8; Non-Textual Materials
Collection, North Carolina State Archives, Raleigh, p. 52; The Rare Book,
Manuscript, and Special Collections Library, Duke University Library, pp. 15,
22, 26; Lorenzo and Thomasina Talley Greene, Papers, Western Historical
Manuscript Collection-Columbia, University of Missouri, p. 100.

Cover Illustration: National Archives

Acknowledgments

John Hope Franklin and Barry Gaspar, two of my colleagues at Duke University, were kind enough to read and make helpful suggestions about this book in the manuscript stage, and I am most grateful to them.

—Robert F. Durden

CONTENTS

Dr. Carter G. Woodson

1

A WELL-DESERVED HONOR

any of the leading African Americans of the nation, along with their white friends and supporters, gathered in Chicago in June 1926. The occasion was the seventeenth annual meeting of the National Association for the Advancement of Colored People, the NAACP. It had been founded in 1909—one hundred years after the birth of Abraham Lincoln—by a mixed group of whites and blacks. They were angry and saddened about the rising tide of white racism and anti-black feeling in the country. The NAACP was the first major organization established to protest and fight against widespread injustice to African Americans.

In 1914, the NAACP began giving an annual award to an African American who had "reached the highest achievement in his [or her] field of activity."[1] The award consisted of a gold medal and a certificate, and it was named for Joel E. Spingarn. He was not only one of the founders of the NAACP, but also one of the leaders in the organization's successful battles in the courts to win greater justice for African Americans.

The awarding of the Spingarn Medal had come to be one of the highlights of the NAACP's annual meeting. Among the earlier winners were such outstanding African Americans as George Washington Carver, a famous scientist; W. E. B. Du Bois, a prominent writer and scholar; and James Weldon Johnson, a poet. Who would win the Spingarn Medal in 1926?

The assembled crowd soon learned that the winner was Carter Godwin Woodson—educator, scholar, and author. Addressing Woodson, the speaker presented the medal as "testimony of the honor in which you are so deservedly held by your fellows of both races. . . ." Woodson's "labors for the truth" had earned him the recognition.[2]

When Carter Woodson won the Spingarn Medal, he was fifty years old and at the peak of his career. The award no doubt meant a great deal to him, for in some ways he led a lonely life. He never married. That meant he lacked the support that being a part of a family can bring. He was so completely wrapped up in his work that, in a way, he was married to his job.

Born in Virginia in 1875, Carter Woodson was the son of parents who had been slaves in Virginia before the Civil War. Their lives had been hard, both before and after the war. In many ways, Carter Woodson's life was hard also. His family, like most African-American families after the Civil War, was poor. There were times when the Woodson family did not even have enough food to eat.[3]

The Woodsons raised young Carter and his brothers and sisters to have strong moral values. They were faithful Baptists and went regularly to church and Sunday school. Along with religion, Carter's parents placed much importance on education. They saw to it that their children took school seriously.

Carter Woodson had to scramble hard to get a proper education. It took a lot of doing, but, in addition to the Spingarn Medal, he ended up with a special claim to fame. He was the first and only African American with once-enslaved parents to receive the highest degree in the field of history that is offered by American universities—the doctor of philosophy, or Ph.D., degree.

Born just ten years after the Civil War ended, Carter Woodson grew up in the lingering shadow of slavery. He also heard many stories about slavery from his parents and grandparents. These stories deeply interested him and helped spark his passion for African-American history.

How did it happen that the son of former slaves won such an important award in 1926? What had Carter G. Woodson done to bring himself this recognition? How did he come to be called the Father of African-American History?

2

In the Shadow of Slavery

hen the Civil War ended in 1865, freedom finally came to the four million or so African Americans who had been slaves in the southern part of the United States. Many of them, like Carter G. Woodson's father, were proud of the part that they had played in winning freedom.

As the years passed, white Americans gradually forgot or ignored the fact that African Americans had helped, in a big way, to win the war for the United States (the North) and to end slavery. African Americans, however, did not forget. Certain leaders, such as Carter G. Woodson, worked hard to have the truth about the African-American role in the Civil War told and written down. They wanted to make sure that someday the full, true story would be known.

Before the Civil War, Woodson's father, James Henry Woodson, was a slave on a plantation on the James River, some seventy-five miles west of Richmond, Virginia. In 1850, the plantation was home to the Woodson family—Carter Woodson's grandfather and grandmother; his father, James Henry; and four other Woodson children—plus fifteen other slaves. The slaves worked at many chores but mostly as field hands in the growing of wheat, corn, oats, and tobacco.[1]

Woodson's father and grandfather were skilled carpenters in addition to being field hands. Since they could make useful things like oxcarts, wagons, and furniture, their owner often hired them out to white neighbors. The neighbors, in turn, paid the owner for the service of his slaves. There is evidence that Woodson's grandfather, father, and uncles were not always mild and obedient slaves. They sometimes resisted when they thought they were being treated unfairly or too harshly.[2]

During the Civil War, James Henry Woodson was hired out to a man who made him dig ditches, among other tasks. He used whatever free time he had, however, to make fish traps and small items of furniture. These he would sell to get pocket change so that he could buy little treats for himself and for his parents.

As slaves, Carter Woodson's father and grandparents often worked as field hands on their owners' tobacco plantation. The tobacco plants above are about ready to have their leaves—starting at the bottom of the plant—picked by hand.

One day the man who had hired James Henry Woodson saw him making some wooden object. The man became angry and tried to whip him. James Henry Woodson hit the man—and then fled back to his owner's place.

Seeing his slave back at home, the owner asked, "What are you doing here at this time of day?" James Henry Woodson explained that he and the man who had hired his services "fell out." That is, they had a quarrel. "Fell out! That's the trouble now! All free! All free," the slave owner declared angrily. "Yes, we are free," James Henry Woodson shot back. "And if you bother me, I'll kill you, another devil."[3]

In speaking out, James Henry Woodson placed himself in danger of harsh punishment. He fled to his cabin, grabbed his best suit of clothes, and ran as fast as he could into the woods. There he changed into his clean clothes and headed eastward toward Richmond. He had heard that there were Union soldiers, "Yankees," in that direction. He hurried on, hoping to run into some northern "friends of freedom."

Finally he saw in the distance some men on horses, men dressed in the dark blue uniforms of the Union army. Waving his white handkerchief, James Henry Woodson approached the Union officer in charge. "Who are you," the officer asked, "a runaway slave?" "Yes sir," James Henry Woodson replied. "I had to escape for my life because to prevent my employer from beating me I had to beat him." "Mount that horse," the officer told Woodson. "Fall in line and come with us. Where is this man that treated you so cruelly?" Woodson told the officer the man's name and that he lived several miles up the river. Then James Henry Woodson led the band of Union soldiers to the man's place. Once there, the soldiers punished the man who had threatened to beat Woodson. The Union soldiers then got Woodson to guide them to various mills and supply storehouses in the region. They quickly scared off the few Confederate (Southern) troops that were around. The Union soldiers took whatever supplies they needed and burned the rest.[4]

For the remaining months of the Civil War, James Henry Woodson served as a scout for the Union army. He stayed on the job until the Confederate general Robert E. Lee surrendered to Union general Ulysses S. Grant in April 1865.

Almost two hundred thousand African Americans fought as soldiers for the Union, the North. James Henry Woodson was not a regular soldier, but he had helped, and both he and his son Carter Woodson had good reason to be proud of that fact.

James Henry Woodson had made his own way to freedom sometime in 1864. The woman whom he would later marry and who would become Carter Woodson's mother was not so lucky. Anne Eliza Riddle was a slave who belonged to the owner of a small farm. His farm was just across the James River from where the

Woodsons lived. Anne Eliza Riddle had light-colored skin because, according to the family story, one of her grandfathers was a white man.

The man who owned the Riddle family, again according to family tradition, was not a harsh or cruel slave owner. Slavery as a system, however, was often cruel despite any good intentions of some slave owners. Among the many harsh features of slavery was that it was against the law for anyone to teach a slave to read and write. Slaveowners feared that if their slaves learned to read they might pick up all sorts of dangerous ideas. Did not the United States Declaration of Independence, for example, speak of all persons being "created equal"? And that they had God-given rights to "life, liberty and the pursuit of happiness"?

The law against teaching slaves to read and write was one that many people, both white and black, ignored. Fortunately for Carter Woodson, his mother was one of the lucky slaves in that respect. Her white mistress taught her to read. This would prove to be one reason that later on, young Carter Woodson would learn to read. He would also have an unusually strong hunger for education.

Another harsh feature of slavery was that slave families were often broken up when an owner sold some of his slaves. Even kind masters sometimes had financial troubles and needed money. In Anne Eliza Riddle's case, her owner decided in the late 1850s, when Anne

Eliza was thirteen or fourteen years old, that he had no choice but to sell her mother and the two youngest boys. Trying to prevent that, Anne Eliza talked the owner into selling her instead, so that her mother could remain with the family. The owner finally agreed, and he sent Anne Eliza to Richmond to be sold. Probably because the owner set too high a price, no one bought her. She later told her son that she felt like an animal as she was moved from the slave pen to the auction block. The owner finally sold her mother and the two youngest sons.[5]

Along with a chance for schooling—for an education—the other thing that the newly freed African Americans most wanted was to own some land. They knew how to farm, and they realized that their best hope for escape from control by white people was to own some land. It was not to be. There were all sorts of rumors and talk toward the end of the Civil War about giving "forty acres and a mule" to the newly freed Africans Americans. It ended up as just talk. Most southern white people did not wish to see the former slaves become landowners. Most northern white people felt the same way or did not much care one way or the other. The northern Republicans claimed the credit for winning the war and freeing the slaves. These Republicans made sure that African-American men got the vote. Land, however, was another matter.

The Woodsons, Riddles, and several million more

like them had to go back to work on white-owned land. They became sharecroppers. While they furnished the labor, the white landowner provided the land, mule, seeds, and other necessities. Then when the crop was harvested, the "cropper"—or laborer—and the landowner each took a share. It was a rickety, make-do system. Crop prices kept falling, and no matter how hard the farmers worked, they stayed in debt. The South after the Civil War became by far the poorest region of the nation. Both whites and African Americans became trapped in a farming system that barely allowed people to live. Unfortunately, this ramshackle system lasted well into the twentieth century.

James Henry Woodson could not make a living as a carpenter after the war, so he tried sharecropping. In 1867, he married Anne Eliza Riddle, and the next year the couple had their first child. James Henry Woodson hoped to make enough money so that he could buy a small farm. His own father finally managed to do that in 1872. In that same year, James Henry Woodson moved his growing family (there were three children by then—Robert Henry, William, and Cora) to West Virginia. It was a new state, which had been created when it separated from Virginia during the Civil War. There were jobs in the West Virginia coal mines and in building railroads.

James Henry and Anne Eliza Woodson worked

hard and saved every cent they could. They finally scraped together just enough money after a few years to buy twenty-one acres of land. It was near his father's farm in Virginia. There, on December 19, 1875, Carter Godwin Woodson was born.

James Henry Woodson finally owned his small bit of land. Making a living, however, was not easy. Carter Woodson later recalled that his mother, with a large family to feed, would come up with enough food for the family's breakfast. But she would still not know where dinner was to come from. He remembered that sometimes during the winter, the family did not have enough to eat. They "would leave the table hungry to go to the woods" to look for wild persimmons that might still be hanging on the tree or lying on the ground.[6] Carter Woodson later said that he often had to go to bed early on Saturday nights so his mother could wash and iron his only garment before Sunday school.

Carter Woodson's parents were faithful Baptists, and the whole family regularly went to church and Sunday school. Also, from an early age the Woodson children learned the importance of education. Young Carter and his brothers and sisters did all sorts of work on the family farm. For four months out of the year, however, they went to a one-room school. The two teachers in the school were Anne Eliza Woodson's brothers, who had earlier learned to read and write.

Faithful Baptists like the Woodson family attended baptism ceremonies like this one, in which adult members of the church affirmed their faith.

These two uncles of Carter Woodson's became his role models.

Carter Woodson later said that his father taught him the most important lessons in life. His father could not read or write, so young Carter often read to him whatever old newspapers they could find. Yet the father was a proud, upright man who insisted upon being treated with respect by blacks and whites alike.[7]

In the 1880s, two of Carter Woodson's older brothers left home to seek work in West Virginia. Young Carter, in the meantime, hired himself out as a farm laborer. He did all sorts of odd jobs to try to help his family. Finally, in 1892, when Carter was about seventeen, he too went to West Virginia. He first worked laying railroad ties but soon went into the coal mines.

Carter Woodson's education took a strange turn as a result of his work as a coal miner. One of his fellow African-American miners was a Civil War veteran who ran a sort of snack bar in his home. There he sold ice cream, watermelons, and other fruit to his fellow African-American miners at the end of the workday. Although Carter Woodson considered the veteran to be highly intelligent, the man could not read. When he learned that Woodson could read, the veteran made a deal: If Woodson would read the newspapers to the miners who gathered in the snack bar after work, he could have free ice cream or fruit or whatever else was available. Woodson jumped at the offer.

The miners got together and subscribed to several African-American newspapers. One, for example, was the *Richmond Planet*, edited by John Mitchell, a prominent leader in Virginia's African-American community. The snack bar owner also had a collection of books in his home. There were books that dealt with the role of African Americans in the Civil War and with other aspects of black history. Whenever some prominent African American came into the area, he would visit the veteran's home and snack bar. In that way, Woodson recalled, "I had the opportunity to learn something about the trials and battles of the Negro for freedom and equality."[8] Woodson and the miners learned a great deal and had lively discussions.

They also subscribed to a number of the white daily newspapers from New York and other cities. They wanted to keep up with events in the country at large and in the world. National and state politics became much more exciting in the 1890s than they had been for many years. Woodson believed, quite correctly, that he was learning a lot about history and economics as a newspaper reader for his fellow miners.[9]

In 1895, after about three years in the coal mines, Woodson moved to Huntington, West Virginia. His parents had already moved there after they gave up on trying to farm for a living. Carter Woodson, age twenty, entered the only high school for African Americans in Huntington.

African-American history was not yet being taught anywhere in the United States. Carter Woodson, however, continued to be highly interested in that subject. His father had taken a job in the railroad yard in Huntington. His foreman was a white Confederate veteran of the Civil War. On many occasions the foreman and Carter Woodson's father discussed the war, with other veterans joining in freely. The discussions were especially lively on Sunday mornings, when work was light.

On Sunday mornings, Woodson's mother would "order" him to take his father "a warm breakfast [in a lunch pail]." Woodson said he grew to welcome the opportunity, for he soon found himself "learning so much about the Civil War from the actual participants." These discussions came to a sudden halt after the Confederate veteran (and foreman) "defended slavery too boldly." Carter Woodson's father got into a fight with the white man, who angrily demanded that Woodson's father be fired. The person in charge refused to do that, but he did order that there be no more discussions of the Civil War.[10]

Carter Woodson went out of his way to meet and learn from African-American veterans of the Civil War. One was a Methodist preacher in Huntington who had succeeded in establishing there an African Methodist Episcopal Church—one that would not be controlled by the white Methodists of the North. A native of

Carter Woodson grew up in rural Virginia, with fields and gently rolling hills like these.

Pittsburgh, Pennsylvania, the preacher had volunteered as a young man to join the Massachusetts 54th Colored Regiment of the Union army. This was the famed African-American regiment commanded by Colonel Robert G. Shaw. In the regiment's attack on Fort Wagner in South Carolina during the Civil War, Shaw and many of the black soldiers were killed. (The 54th and the attack on Fort Wagner would much later, in the 1990s, be featured in the movie *Glory*.) The Pennsylvanian was taken prisoner and held for the rest of the war. "The Negro prisoners," he told Woodson, "were poorly clad, poorly fed, and sometimes all but starved."[11] At times, he said, they had so little meat to eat that they gnawed on the leather of old shoes and even sank to eating dog meat.

Another veteran told Woodson of making the sad discovery that "the Union soldiers were about as much prejudiced against the Negro soldiers as were the Confederates." This veteran had insisted on equal treatment and equal pay. He finally became so disgusted, however, that he and some of his fellow African Americans resigned from the army.[12]

From his parents and grandparents, Woodson had learned a great deal about slavery. From his father and the friends he made in the coal mine, as well as from later friends in Huntington, he learned much about the African-American role in the Civil War. Woodson carefully stored up in his mind all that he had learned about slavery and the Civil War. Those facts and ideas were quite different from what was in the books that white historians were then writing. One of Woodson's great goals in life would be to have the African-American view of slavery and the Civil War told—and not just told, but written about carefully and with plenty of proof, evidence that could not be ignored.

3

STUDENT, TEACHER, TRAVELER

ll the time that Carter Woodson was storing up rich, important information about slavery and the Civil War, he was also working hard to complete his education. He finished four years of high school work in two years. Then, in the fall of 1897, he enrolled at Berea College in Kentucky.

Berea was an unusual college. It had been started in 1858, a few years before the Civil War, by an abolitionist, a strong foe of slavery. John G. Fee, a white Kentuckian, was determined that African Americans should have the opportunity for an education. During and long after the Civil War, Berea operated as an integrated, or racially mixed, college. Fee's great hope was that there be about equal numbers of black and white students. Scholarships and jobs on campus allowed poor people like Woodson to attend Berea.

By the time Woodson got there, however, Berea's open door to African Americans was already beginning to close. White racism and anti-black activities had increased all across the nation in the 1890s and early 1900s.[1] An elaborate system of "Jim Crow segregation" quickly developed in the South in the years just before and after 1900: New state and city laws required that the races be kept separate—or segregated—in schools, theaters, restaurants, and just about everywhere else. Then the white Democrats in the southern states found a variety of ways to deny the vote to African-American men. From about 1800 until the end of the Civil War, the South differed from the rest of the nation by clinging so strongly to slavery. After 1900, the South was again different because of the widespread and strict Jim Crow system of laws.

In 1900, most African Americans—around 90 percent—still lived in the South. The minority who lived in the North also faced problems from white prejudice. In the North there were no formal laws requiring segregation. It was just the custom in most parts of the North to keep the races separate.

At Berea, this national trend toward denying equal treatment to African Americans resulted in a shrinking

Berea College's classroom-administration building (Lincoln Hall, left) and the science building (right), as they looked around 1900, when Woodson was there.

number of blacks being admitted to the college. In 1892, a little more than 50 percent of the students were African Americans. By 1903, when Woodson graduated, the number had been reduced to about 16 percent. The next year, 1904, the state government of Kentucky enacted a law requiring Berea to stop admitting African Americans entirely.[2]

Woodson entered college in 1897, but he did not have enough money to stay at Berea for his full freshman year. He dropped out to teach at a school that black miners had started for their children in a small town in West Virginia. In 1900, he became the principal at the high school for African Americans that he had attended in Huntington, West Virginia. He returned to Berea on a part-time basis in 1901 and later attended a summer session at the University of Chicago. Finally, by 1903, he had completed enough courses to graduate from Berea. Though he had to scramble to do it, he was determined to get the best education that he could find.

Going to college was one way to become educated. Traveling, especially to foreign counties, was another. In 1903, Woodson, age twenty-eight, seized an opportunity to travel to a faraway country: the Philippine Islands. In 1898, the United States had gone to war with Spain to help the Cubans win their freedom from Spain. That was done in short order. The United States did not stop there, however. It ended up forcing Spain to turn over to the United States the Spanish colonies of Puerto Rico in the Atlantic Ocean and the faraway Philippine Islands in the Pacific Ocean.

Long ruled by Spain, many of the Filipino people spoke Spanish in addition to their native language. The United States government, as the new ruler of the islands, wanted to start schools and teach English to the people. Woodson decided to go to the Philippines to teach English. Aside from the chance to travel, the pay also attracted Woodson. As a school principal he earned only $65 per month. In the Philippines he could make $100 a month, which was a good salary in that day.[3]

After a long ocean voyage to Hong Kong, he continued on to Manila, the capital of the Philippines. Then Woodson began his new work. It was not easy. He was first assigned to a school in a small town near Manila. He spoke no Spanish, and his students spoke no English. But in tough situations people learn to cope, to make do. So Woodson spent his days teaching English, health, and some farming skills. His nights and any free time he had were spent studying Spanish and some French. He took courses in those languages through the mail. They were called correspondence courses and were offered by the University of Chicago. Within a year, Woodson spoke and wrote Spanish well.

The courses that Woodson took through the mail forced him to do a lot of reading. He had to write long,

Carter G. Woodson

In the Philippines, Carter Woodson taught English to Filipino students at a school run by the United States government.

detailed answers to many questions. Between his teaching and his correspondence courses, Woodson had little time for fun and games. He was a serious, hard-working person who was hungry for more education.

In addition to studying Spanish and French, he took courses in ancient and modern European history. Woodson was establishing a pattern of living alone and working hard. He taught school each day and then became a student himself each night and on the weekends.

After more than two years of teaching in the Philippines, Woodson returned to the United States to visit his parents. When he became ill at home, he resigned from his job as a teacher in the Philippines. He still wanted to travel, however. Using money he had managed to save, he set off in 1907 on a trip that took him to many foreign places. He visited cities in Asia, Africa, and Europe.

Through his studying and travels, Woodson had come to believe that historians did not pay enough attention to African history. This was an idea that Woodson shared with W. E. B. Du Bois, one of the most prominent African-American leaders of the time. Like Du Bois, Woodson also believed that a certain number of African Americans—what Du Bois called "the talented tenth"—should go to the best colleges they could. They could then become leaders in the African-American community. Woodson, however, probably knew the actual conditions of rural blacks in the South better than Du Bois did. Therefore Woodson also agreed with Booker T. Washington, another important African-American leader, that many poor blacks in the rural South needed training for jobs—training in vocations.[4]

On his travels in so many foreign countries, Woodson was not a typical tourist. He did see many famous sights, but it was the foreign schools and their teaching methods that were of special interest to him. He visited libraries and tried to meet as many learned scholars as he could. In Paris, France, Woodson did research in the National Library. He attended lectures at the University of Paris and met some of the out-standing history professors in France.

He came back to the United States in the fall of 1907. Now he was ready to continue his formal education. This time it would be done at two of the top universities in the country.

4

MAKING HISTORY
WITH A PH.D.

At one point, Woodson's parents had hoped that he would become a preacher. As a young schoolteacher and principal in Huntington, West Virginia, Woodson did preach at least once in the Baptist church.[1] His experiences at Berea College and in the Philippines, however, led him to choose a career as teacher. He did not want to be just an ordinary teacher—he wanted to be a scholar, that is, a teacher who also writes learned books and articles. He chose history as the field in which he wished to work.

The type of high-level graduate training in research methods that Woodson set out to obtain in

1907 was still fairly new in the United States. Not until the last quarter of the nineteenth century—that is, after 1875 (the year Woodson was born)—did certain strong American colleges begin to change themselves into research universities. This select group of top universities stressed research as one of the primary tasks of the professors. They were expected to blaze new trails in all the important fields of learning. They wanted to make new discoveries and extend the boundaries of knowledge. The professors were also expected to train the most advanced students, the graduate students, to do research. This training usually came after four years of college work. The reward at the end was the highest degree offered by the universities, the doctor of philosophy, or Ph.D., degree. It was a new degree offered only by universities that emphasized research.

At first the research universities, and then later the stronger four-year colleges, began to expect their faculty members to have the Ph.D. degree. Earning this degree was the ambitious goal that Carter Woodson set for himself.

Woodson had attended a summer session at the University of Chicago and had taken correspondence courses from there. His decision to do graduate work there was a natural one. The officials at the University of Chicago admitted Woodson, but they said that he needed to do more undergraduate work to be better prepared for the advanced-level program. Woodson buckled down and took both undergraduate and graduate courses at the same time.[2]

Before he could try for the Ph.D. degree, Woodson had to earn a master of arts (M.A.) degree. For that, in addition to taking classes for a year, he had to write a thesis. This was a long, careful research paper—like a short book actually—that would show his ability to do research and to present his findings in an organized, acceptable manner.

For the subject of his master's thesis, Woodson at first wanted to write about some aspect of the history of black churches. This did not work out. It is unclear whether he could not find enough material on the subject in Chicago or his professors did not approve of the topic. He ended up writing a thesis on a topic in European history. For this, he was helped by his knowledge of the French language and some work he had done in the National Library in Paris. Successfully over the first hurdle, he received both another undergraduate degree and a master's degree from the University of Chicago in 1908.

For the next and highest degree, the Ph.D., Woodson chose to go to Harvard University. The oldest college in the nation, it had quickly become one of the strongest of the new research universities. In the fall of 1908, Harvard accepted Woodson as a graduate student. Most American universities at that time would not admit African Americans. If Woodson expected to find a warm, encouraging reception at Harvard, he was soon disappointed.

Woodson quickly learned that one of his major professors in American history at Harvard, a man named Edward Channing, believed that African Americans had no special history. In the graduate class he taught, Channing downplayed any black role in the American Revolution, the Civil War, or American history in general. When Woodson tried to argue otherwise, Channing declared that Woodson should do research to prove that African Americans had a history.[3]

Turned off by Channing's attitude, Woodson turned to another well-known professor of American history at Harvard, Albert Bushnell Hart. Although Hart saw blacks as an inferior race, he thought they deserved the benefits of education. Hart became Woodson's supervisor, or major professor.

Hart helped train Woodson to do careful research. Woodson was learning to assemble factual material and then to organize it and present it in such a way that people could understand it. He agreed with Hart's belief that historians should share their findings with the general public. The two men also agreed that when it was possible to talk with people who had some direct, firsthand knowledge of past events, that type of oral or spoken history could be valuable. When carefully

When Carter Woodson was a student at Harvard, he spent many
hours in Gore Hall at the university library.

considered, that type of information could be used alongside old letters, newspapers, and other written sources as a basis for history.[4]

Because Woodson already had his master's degree from the University of Chicago, he had hoped that he could obtain the Ph.D. fairly quickly. He completed a year of classes in European and American history at Harvard, but there were two more hurdles he had to jump: (1) general or qualifying examinations on all of his work in both European and American history; and (2) a doctoral dissertation, a report that was as long as a sizable book. It had to be original work on a subject that no one had already covered and had to be based on firsthand sources. A committee of the senior professors in Harvard's history department would have to accept and approve the dissertation. Then Woodson would, finally, have the Ph.D. It was a long, tricky process. In the end, persistence—simply sticking to the job and not giving up—counted a lot toward success.

Woodson needed at least another year at Harvard. He was not awarded a fellowship that would pay for a second year, however. His own savings gone, he considered giving up and returning to the Philippines to teach. He also applied for a teaching job in Washington, D.C.

If Woodson had gone back to the Philippines, it would probably have meant the end of his hopes for a

Ph.D. from Harvard. He would be too far away to return for the special examinations he had to take. Also, in the Philippines he would not be able to do any of the necessary research for a dissertation.

Still, Woodson began to prepare for his return to the Philippines. Almost at the last minute, in July 1909, he learned that he could have a teaching job in the public schools of Washington, D.C., if he wanted it. He quickly decided to accept. In Washington, he could use the splendid Library of Congress for both study and research. He would not, after all, have to give up on his goal of earning a Ph.D. in history. He had long ago learned to cram extra work into his evenings and weekends.

In Washington, Woodson at first taught at a manual-training high school for students who did not plan to go on to college. This was not an academically demanding school. In 1911, however, Woodson was transferred to M Street High School. It was the best high school for African Americans in the nation's capital. Later it was renamed the Paul Laurence Dunbar High School after the celebrated African-American poet. It became widely recognized as the city's leading school for African-American students who were preparing for college.[5]

For six years—from the fall of 1911 until the end of 1917—Woodson taught at the M Street High School. He taught American history, French, Spanish, and

English. A former student recalled that Woodson had a formal air about him but that he also had a sparkle in his eyes. Another student remembered that when classes changed, Woodson would stand in the hallway outside his classroom. His mere presence encouraged proper behavior among the students passing in the hallways.[6]

The dignified teacher whom the students remembered was slim and of medium height. He had large, dark brown eyes, and dark, curly hair framed his handsome face.

Woodson's high school students may not have known it, but he no doubt studied and worked much harder than they did. This was because all during his early years as a teacher in Washington, he was preparing for the special examinations he still had to take at Harvard. He was also doing the research for his dissertation, and he spent countless hours in the Library of Congress.

Early in 1910, Woodson successfully passed the general examination in European history. The Harvard professors questioned him in several different areas of European history, and Woodson came through well. Woodson had more trouble in American history. He failed the general examination in that field the first time he took it. On the second try, he passed.

The last hurdle he had to get across for the Ph.D.

may have been the toughest. For his doctoral dissertation, Woodson chose to write about the formation of the state of West Virginia during the Civil War. He did much research on the subject in the Library of Congress. During the summers, he visited his family in West Virginia and did additional research there. He carefully read and took notes on the information in old newspapers, official state records, and collections of the letters of various leading West Virginians in the Civil War era.

Despite all of Woodson's labors, the Harvard professors did not approve his dissertation at first. Woodson was no doubt discouraged, but he was also determined to keep trying. He did additional research and made many changes in his long study. In April 1912, the professors approved Woodson's dissertation. He then received the Ph.D. degree in history, becoming the first and only African American with once-enslaved parents to have that distinction.

By the time Woodson reached his academic goal, he was thirty-six years old. He had been teaching school, in the United States and in the Philippines, for a dozen or so years. It had been a long, hard pull, but Carter Woodson had persisted. He had accomplished what he set out to do.

For Woodson, obtaining the Ph.D. was not an end but a beginning. It was a tool that he could use to demonstrate that African Americans had a special history. He would soon play a leading role in establishing that fact. It would eventually result in a truer, broader type of American history. Carter Woodson would not live to see the full realization of his dream, but his work provided an important foundation.

5

A Mission to
Educate Others

or Carter Woodson and other educated
African Americans like him, a strange and
upsetting thing happened in the early
1900s: Their understanding of the nation's past grew
more and more different from that of most white
Americans.

Take the Civil War, for example. Woodson learned
early from his father that African Americans helped
the North win the war and thus end slavery. Later, as
Woodson continued his education, he read pioneering
histories of the black soldiers in the Union army. One
example of the kind of book that he probably read and

that he and his fellow coal miners had discussed back in the 1890s would be *A History of the Negro Troops in the War of the Rebellion, 1861–1865*. It was written by a pioneering African-American historian, George Washington Williams, and published in 1887.

White Americans, however, largely ignored books by black Americans such as Williams. By the early 1900s, the African-American role in the Civil War was either forgotten or ignored by most whites. So much was this the case that a white historian could write as follows in the 1920s:

> . . . the American negroes are the only people in the history of the world, so far as I know, that ever became free without any effort of their own. . . . They twanged banjos around the railroad stations, sang melodious spirituals, and believed that some Yankee would soon come along and give each of them forty acres of land and a mule.[1]

Twanged banjos, indeed. Woodson knew that the above statement was untrue. He knew so from conversations with African Americans who had fought in the war and from knowledge gained from books. He knew that the statement slandered his race. Nevertheless, it was typical of the "best" white history of the time.

Concerning slavery itself, white historians were presenting a picture that was far different from what Woodson had learned directly from his once-enslaved parents and grandparents. It was not surprising, of course, that southern whites would view slavery

These African-American soldiers in Company E, 4th U.S.
Colored Infantry, fought for the Union army (the North) in the
Civil War. Carter Woodson fought all of his adult life to have
their role in the war—and that of thousands of other African-
American soldiers like them—recognized by historians.

through rose-colored glasses. Through novels and short stories, many southern writers found a large national audience eager to swallow a sugar-coated version of slavery. What was more disturbing to Woodson, however, was that the leading white historian of slavery, Ulrich B. Phillips, also portrayed it as a basically kind and humane institution. As white southerners so much wanted to believe, this prominent historian even suggested that most African Americans had been happy and content as slaves.

The twelve years after the Civil War were known as the Reconstruction Era. This period of history also came to be understood differently by white and black Americans. By the time Woodson was an adult teacher and scholar, most people had come to accept the southern viewpoint about Reconstruction. That is, most northern whites agreed with southern whites that the Republicans had made a sad mistake after the war when they gave the vote to African-American men. The southern Democrats, those who belonged to "the white man's party," were now seen as the heroes of the Reconstruction Era. Even the Ku Klux Klan, the white terrorist organization that helped the southern Democrats, had come to be viewed as having been necessary and useful.

Woodson's frustration and anger about what he saw as huge untruths and distortions grew. For scholars to write misleading books was bad enough, but at least they reached only a limited audience. Then, in 1915, the most talked-about and important movie that Hollywood had made up to that time came out. It was D. W. Griffith's *The Birth of a Nation*, a movie about the Civil War and Reconstruction. Griffith was a pioneering genius in the art of moviemaking. The film was based on best-selling novels by a very racist white southerner, Thomas Dixon, Jr. *The Birth of a Nation* was a silent movie with captions that told what the actors were saying. In the larger cities, a full orchestra provided powerful music to accompany the film. In the smaller places, someone played an organ or a piano to set the mood and heighten the effect of the picture.

Americans flocked to see *The Birth of a Nation* as they had to no other movie before it. President Woodrow Wilson had it shown in the White House. The fact that the movie gave a rosy view of slavery did not bother most white viewers. African Americans were portrayed in the film as either happy-go-lucky, childlike creatures or as mean brutes intent on attacking white women.[2]

Leading African Americans and their few white allies protested and marched against the showing of *The Birth of a Nation*. The protests were in vain, however. Many millions of Americans—as well as people in other parts of the world—believed the movie's version of history. Much later, in 1939, another very popular movie about the same subject, *Gone with the Wind*, would have a similar impact.

Thomas Dixon, Jr., was the author of several racist novels about the Civil War and Reconstruction Era. These best-sellers were the basis for a hugely popular silent movie, *The Birth of a Nation.*

Woodson spent much of the summer of 1915 in Chicago. He had gone there to participate in the Exposition of Negro Progress, which marked the fiftieth anniversary of freedom for African Americans. Woodson set up a booth to sell African-American history books and photographs of such famous figures as Frederick Douglass and Sojourner Truth, two leading abolitionists; and poet Paul Lawrence Dunbar. Ever studious, Woodson also carried a suitcase full of books and notes, for he planned to do research and to write while in Chicago.[3]

In the evenings at the black YMCA where he rented a room, Woodson also took part in lively discussions. He and some other well-educated African Americans talked about politics, relations between blacks and whites, and—Woodson's favorite topic—black history. They also criticized *The Birth of a Nation* and its grossly inaccurate view of African Americans.

These conversations inspired Woodson: Why should there not be an organization of African Americans—along with any sympathetic whites who wished to join—to promote African-American history? White historians were either ignoring the black role in the building of the nation or presenting incorrect, racist versions of that role. African Americans would have to speak up and make known their own history.

The National Association for the Advancement of Colored People (NAACP), established in 1909, was intended by its black and white founders to focus on the present. African Americans were being denied justice and their legal rights under the United States Constitution. The NAACP, therefore, had set out to use the courts and other peaceful methods to fight back.

Another biracial organization, the National Urban League, had been started in 1911. Its primary purpose was to help African Americans living in cities find jobs and housing. So while the NAACP operated largely in the political and legal arena, the National Urban League had an economic mission. These organizations provided models for Woodson.[4]

Woodson and his friends in Chicago first talked about starting a "Historical Alliance." They ended up, however, establishing, on September 9, 1915, the Association for the Study of Negro Life and History. The next month, when Woodson returned to Washington, he went to the proper government office to have the new association legally chartered.

In starting these national organizations, Woodson and the other founders were doing something typically American. A brilliant young Frenchman named Alexis de Tocqueville had come to study the United States back in the 1830s. Andrew Jackson was president then, and the nation was in its robust adolescence. Tocqueville wrote a book about the United States when he returned to France. He titled it *Democracy in America*, and many people consider it the

This cartoon attacking Thomas Dixon, Jr., appeared in the NAACP's magazine, the *Crisis,* in October 1915. Like Carter Woodson, the National Association for the Advancement of Colored People was outraged by the untrue portrayal of African Americans in *The Birth of a Nation.*

best book that has ever been written about the United States.

Among the many sharp observations that Tocqueville made, one thing that particularly struck him was that the Americans were always as busy as beavers forming voluntary associations. They organized groups to do things for the community—such as starting a public library or beginning a series of musical concerts. They organized themselves on the local level and on the national level. Unlike people in Europe, the Americans, according to Tocqueville, did not sit around waiting for the government or the official, state-sponsored church (as in Europe) to do everything. Tocqueville thought it admirable that Americans worked together to get things done and to bring about all sorts of reforms and changes in society.

Before the Civil War, only the small minority of African Americans who were in the North were free to form voluntary associations. They began to do that quite early, however. After the war, African Americans in the South also began eagerly to form their own associations and clubs. The most important voluntary associations for the newly freed blacks were, of course, their own separate churches. In time African Americans across the nation formed various other local organizations such as historical, musical, literary, and burial societies. The NAACP, the National Urban League, and Woodson's Association for the Study of

Negro Life and History were all national in scope, biracial, and deeply American.

In addition to getting local branches of the new association started, Woodson wanted the association to sponsor a scholarly journal. This was one of his primary goals. He wanted to demonstrate, once and for all, that African Americans had a history. It could be presented in the same careful, scientific, or scholarly manner as any other type of history. There was, however, no money for starting such a journal. Woodson borrowed $400 and used the money to bring out the first issue of the *Journal of Negro History* in January 1916.[5]

The *Journal of Negro History* was published four times a year. It carried carefully footnoted articles about a wide range of topics. The articles dealt with black people in North America and in the Caribbean and South America. Since Woodson recognized that the African past was important for American blacks, he also made sure that some articles dealt with Africa.

The journal carried book reviews, with Woodson selecting the books and writing many of the reviews himself. Even more than most other historical journals, Woodson's journal emphasized documents. These were the raw materials of history—the sources on which books and articles were based. Woodson collected letters written by white and black abolitionists, diaries, and other types of records touching on slavery and African-American life. One remarkable item that he discovered was a diary kept by an African-American family beginning in 1794.

By including many of these documents in the journal, Woodson made them available to other historians. In addition, while most historians were still focused on important people and especially on political leaders, Woodson collected records of the common people. Beginning in 1920 and continuing for several years, the *Journal of Negro History* had a section called "Undistinguished Negroes."

Later Woodson published letters from ordinary persons about living conditions in the South or about job opportunities in the North. He was ahead of his time in recognizing the value of such material. Not until the 1960s and after would other historians turn to such sources for social history about the lives of plain folk.

Before Woodson died, he gave his vast collection of documentary material to the Library of Congress. "If all of his other scholarly contributions were placed aside," one of his biographers has written, "the over five thousand items that he amassed and later turned over to the Library of Congress for the use of others, would mark him for distinction."[6]

With the *Journal of Negro History* well under way, Woodson turned to the job of building up the Association for the Study of Negro Life and History. It held its first large meeting in Washington, D.C., in

August 1917. Many persons seriously interested in the study of Negro history were present. These included government officials, presidents of and professors in black colleges, and white philanthropists—people who donate money to various causes. This last group was especially important, for Woodson looked to them for financial support of the journal and other association activities.

Woodson explained to the group that one of the primary purposes of the association was "to save the records of the black race." In that way African Americans would avoid the sad fate of the American Indians. They had left, Woodson declared, "no written account of [their] thoughts, feelings, aspirations, and achievements."[7]

Part of Woodson's plan was to hire young historians who could tackle special research projects in black history. That too would take money, so Woodson was especially pleased that wealthy white friends of the African-American race attended the Washington meeting. Among them were George Foster Peabody and Julius Rosenwald. A rich Chicagoan, Rosenwald would prove to be one of Woodson's most important supporters. A generous friend of many black causes, Rosenwald took a special interest in helping to build public schools for African Americans in the South. Rosenwald praised the *Journal of Negro History* and promised to give $400 a year to help pay for it.

Like the NAACP and the National Urban League, Woodson sought to involve whites in his association. He arranged to have Rosenwald and other prominent whites added to the black members of the executive or governing committee of the association. At this point, according to one of Woodson's biographers, he was "courting any and all whites who could and would aid him." At the same time, he seemed wary of having prominent blacks on the executive committee. "This seems to indicate that from the beginning Woodson was anxious to maintain absolute control over the organization."[8]

By the end of 1916, Woodson and his allies had managed to line up almost one thousand subscribers to the journal. Still, the total amount of money raised was only $1,400. Woodson had already run up a debt of $1,100, so more money was clearly going to be needed. By writing many letters and visiting potential donors, Woodson was able to scrape together enough support each year to keep the journal going. What he really wanted and needed was a sizable grant of money that could serve as an endowment for the journal and the association. That is, if a sizable sum of money were invested as an endowment, there would be annual income from the investment. That annual income would provide a sound footing for both the journal and the association.

Woodson proved unable to secure the endowment.

The main reason was that he basically wanted to run a one-man operation. Many people, both black and white, recognized the great value of the *Journal of Negro History*. The Association for the Study of Negro Life and History grew steadily as branches were formed in many of the nation's cities. In 1919, Woodson hired a field agent to help organize local history clubs. What would happen to the journal and the association, however, if anything should happen to Woodson? If he became ill or if he should die, would the activities that he had started just wither away? These were the tough questions asked by the foundations supported by the white philanthropists. Seeing no clear answers to the questions, they held back on money for an endowment.

Woodson received no salary for editing the journal and directing the association. He still earned his living as a high school teacher, and for one year as a high school principal. He even used some of his own money to keep the journal going.

One possible solution to the problem was briefly discussed in 1917. From the beginning of the NAACP, W. E. B. Du Bois was the editor of its important magazine, the *Crisis*. By 1918, the magazine's circulation had reached one hundred thousand readers per month. One well-to-do white supporter of the NAACP wanted the organization to help Woodson. Du Bois agreed to offer Woodson a relationship with the *Crisis*:

Woodson would get office space and a small salary, and the *Journal of Negro History* would be published by the NAACP, instead of by Woodson's association. Woodson considered the offer, but turned it down. He did not wish to give up his independence and work under the direction of Du Bois.[9]

Finally, in 1919, a door opened to Woodson that held great promise, both for him personally and for his beloved journal and association. Howard University in Washington, D.C., invited him to become the dean of its School of Liberal Arts and the first director of Howard's new graduate program in history. Howard was one of a group of schools for newly freed African Americans that had been established soon after the Civil War. After World War I, Howard had rising ambitions and a new white president. It hoped to begin to move in the direction of becoming a research university. None of the African-American colleges and universities had yet found the large amounts of money needed to achieve such a change.

In many ways, the position was ideal for Woodson. His advanced training at the University of Chicago and Harvard made him one of a still small group of African Americans with the Ph.D. degree. Keen about doing historical research himself, he wanted to train younger historians and had many excellent topics in mind. In 1915, he had published his first book, *The Education of the Negro Prior to 1861*. There would be

W. E. B. Du Bois was a prominent African-American leader and author. Woodson and Du Bois were not friends, but Woodson shared Du Bois's belief in the importance of education for African Americans.

quite a few later books, but even that first one had given him a certain standing in the historical profession. Finally, by belonging to the faculty at Howard, Woodson would have an institutional connection for the *Journal of Negro History*. That was something that many of its—and Woodson's—supporters believed to be important.

The question was, could Woodson work as part of a team? He had scrambled long and hard to get his education. He had found something important to do with his life: establish the *Journal of Negro History* and the Association for the Study of Negro Life and History. Could he now manage to combine those great passions with a type of advanced-level teaching that would be new to him? He had proved to be a hard worker, but could he also work under the authority of someone else?

6

LAUNCHING
NEGRO HISTORY
WEEK

he answer to the question of whether Carter Woodson could be happy working under someone else is that he could not. That was especially true if he disliked or lacked respect for the person under whom he was supposed to work. The new position at Howard University offered him a valuable opportunity to use his many talents. He also had a chance to help strengthen the university in a key area—graduate work in history. Woodson, however, remained in the job only one year.

He got off to a good start in the fall of 1919.

Woodson led in organizing Howard's first faculty committee on graduate study. In the history department he developed a new program of study offering a master of arts degree in the history and culture of the Negro.[1]

While four other historians covered European, Latin American, and African history, Woodson taught all the courses in United States history. He also introduced the first full-fledged course in African-American history taught at Howard. Earlier, there had been a lecture series on black history. Charles H. Wesley, who had taught at Howard since 1913, had prepared courses in African-American history, but they were not taught. The trustees of the university approved the offering of courses in the field only after Woodson's appointment. This was probably because he was then the only faculty member to have a Ph.D. in history.[2]

In Woodson's upper-level teaching, he carefully followed the same system that he had found earlier at Harvard. Working closely with Woodson, each student had to select a topic to research. Students had to use firsthand sources, and not just textbooks or books written by other historians. Keeping at least a *B* average, each had to give an oral report to the class and write a long, scholarly report.

Woodson told his five graduate students at the outset that they would have to be serious about their work. (He always was about his!) He suggested that they plan to spend six hours a day in the library. Perhaps he scared them, for of the five students who began the seminar course, only one actually completed it. That student stuck it out, he later explained, because he admired and respected Woodson. The respect must have been mutual, for Woodson published the student's master's thesis as an article in the *Journal of Negro History*.[3]

In the long run, Woodson's high standards would probably have helped Howard University. He got into trouble, though, with the university's president. The trouble was as much or more the president's fault as Woodson's. But Woodson, not the president, lost his job.

The difficulty began about a small matter. Howard had a daily chapel service. Attendance by the faculty was not required. The president, however, wanted to know which faculty members went to the service. He asked Woodson to check and report to him about the matter. This was a task that Woodson, understandably, did not like.

A more serious problem arose when the president ordered a certain book removed from Howard's library. This was soon after the Communists had captured power in Russia during the revolution there. In the United States, fear and hatred of Communists grew quite strong around 1919–1920. It was a time that came to be known as the "Red Scare," since Communists were also called "Reds." A United States senator, Reed Smoot, objected to the Howard library's having a particular book about the Soviets. The senator demanded that the book be removed. Since Howard depended heavily on money from the federal government, the nervous university president quickly ordered the book's removal.

Free speech—whether written or spoken—is protected in the United States by the Constitution. At colleges and universities, free speech is especially important and is often termed academic freedom. Woodson argued, correctly, that both the senator and Howard's president had stomped on academic freedom by having the book removed from the library. Woodson could not keep silent. He wrote a letter to the Washington *Star* attacking Howard's president for his role in the matter. Woodson suggested that Howard University would be better off without the government's meddling in its affairs.

When the newspaper published Woodson's letter, Howard's president summoned Woodson to his office. The meeting was stormy. After one or two other disagreements with the president, Woodson considered resigning from his job. One of his old friends tried to persuade Woodson to hang on. The friend argued that strong black scholars, like Woodson, were needed at Howard. For the sake of the students and the faculty, Woodson should rise above the quarrel. "Think it all over, go to church, sing some of the good old hymns you used to sing, take a stroll in the park to try to forget the world," the friend wrote.[4]

Woodson may have at first taken the friend's advice to heart. He did write a peacemaking letter to the president, and he asked for another meeting. That meeting did not settle the trouble. The trustees of Howard backed the president and fired Woodson as the academic year ended. A few years later, the president was forced to resign. That, however, was too late to help Woodson. He had burned his bridges at Howard University.

Desperate about his need to make a living, Woodson, in the spring of 1920, asked the NAACP to take over the *Journal of Negro History* and pay him a salary to edit it. By this time, the NAACP was having some money troubles of its own and turned Woodson down.

Fortunately for Woodson, a new job soon came his way. Earlier he had been asked to become the president of an African-American college, the West Virginia Collegiate Institute. Woodson had rejected that offer for two main reasons: First, he thought that being a college president would leave him too little time to do his own research and to edit the *Journal of Negro History*. Second, he wanted to remain in Washington to direct and promote the Association for the Study of Negro Life and History. Woodson recommended a friend for the presidency, and the friend got the job. Now, as a nice return favor, the friend, who was president of the West Virginia Collegiate Institute, invited Woodson to become dean of the college department at a salary of $2,700 a year. Woodson promptly and gratefully accepted the offer.[5]

During his one year at Howard and two years at West Virginia Collegiate Institute, Woodson never for a moment lost sight of his main purpose in life. That was to advance the cause of African-American history. He wanted to do this through his own research and writings, through the *Journal of Negro History*, and through the Association for the Study of Negro Life and History. Even before he left Howard, he came up with another activity that would help the cause of African-American history.

In 1921, Woodson started Associated Publishers, a book publishing company, to get books on African-American history on the market. He and others who supported the venture saw a real need for the new company. In Woodson's own case, he recalled submitting his first book, *The Education of the Negro Prior to 1861*, to a New York publishing firm. The New York firm would not publish the book unless Woodson put up his own money to have it printed and distributed. The major publishing firms, all owned by whites, believed that books written by blacks would not sell. That was especially true, the publishers thought, if the books were scholarly. Woodson started Associated Publishers to give black scholars an opportunity to get their books in print. He also hoped that the new company would make money that could help support other activities of the Association for the Study of Negro Life and History. As it turned out, Woodson's Associated Publishers did issue many books by black scholars. Unfortunately, the company never made much money.[6]

During Woodson's year at Howard and after he began his job in West Virginia, he continually beat the bushes trying to raise money to support the journal and the association. In 1919, he had set out to raise $2,000 by appealing to readers of the *Journal of Negro History* as well as to a group of prominent whites and blacks. Within a few months, he raised $1,200. Writing about this to an African-American army officer, Woodson explained: "You may be surprised to learn that every penny of the $1,200 already pledged has come from white persons." Woodson quickly added that he understood that most blacks at that time had little or no money to spare. He was trying, however, to nudge the black army officer into contributing. The effort succeeded, though the officer's contribution was a small one.[7]

Woodson's never-ending efforts to raise money finally paid off. He did not get the large, long-range endowment that he wanted for the journal. In 1921, however, the Carnegie Foundation in New York, one of the oldest and largest philanthropic organizations, gave Woodson $25,000 to support his work in African-American history: Woodson would get $5,000 a year for five years. Woodson had still not linked the journal to a college or university. The Carnegie Foundation by no means just turned Woodson loose to use its money however he might wish. He had to send his budget telling how the money was to be spent, along with regular reports, to a prominent historian. This white historian, J. Franklin Jameson, was a leading figure in the profession and directed the American Historical Association.

The grant was a godsend. For the first time since he had established the association and the journal, Woodson could see ahead—at least for five years. He decided to give up his job in West Virginia. He would devote full time to the journal, the association, the new publishing company, and his own research. Starting in 1922, Woodson for the first time received a salary for his work in African-American history. In that same year, Woodson had Associated Publishers buy a three-story brick house on Ninth Street in Washington. Woodson borrowed the $2,750 needed to buy the house and had to make a down payment of only $10.[8] The Association for the Study of Negro Life and History finally had permanent headquarters. Woodson also had a home, for he used the third floor of the house as his residence for the rest of his life.

The Carnegie Foundation also required Woodson to employ a business manager for the *Journal of Negro History* and the association. Woodson hired a young African-American graduate of Cornell University but fired him a year later. As one of Woodson's biographers noted, he "had no desire to share his organization with another." This "weakness on Woodson's part was to cause him considerable difficulty in the future."[9]

According to the fired business manager, Woodson treated him harshly. Woodson sent him to some very poor African-American schools in the South. The business manager was supposed to sell the journal to the schools. In many cases, these schools had no money, not even for food. In one school in Tennessee, the entire library consisted of forty hymn books. The business manager shared a meal there with the teachers and students. This pitiful meal consisted of cornmeal and milk.

The business manager described Woodson as "a hard man to get along with." He thought that Woodson had been forced to "scuffle" so much for his own education that the struggle had hardened him. "If I had to characterize Dr. Woodson in those days," the business manager later said, "I would say he was a lonely man; never had any close friend; never had anyone he could confide in." Only a few people

Carter G. Woodson

Always independent in thought and action, Carter Woodson jumped at the chance to devote all of his time and energy to the study and promotion of African-American history.

"could see he had a good heart beneath a brusque exterior."[10]

Although Woodson clearly had problems in working with other people, he was still someone who got a great deal of work done by himself. The first book published by Associated Publishers turned out to be Woodson's own *History of the Negro Church* (1922). It was one of his most important and useful books and was on a subject that was close to Woodson's heart. The actual printing of the book was done by a firm in New York. Woodson gave lengthy, precise instructions to the printer about how the book and its illustrations were to be produced. In making a book, printers prepare what are known as page proofs. They are carefully read by both the author and other "proof readers" to get rid of printing errors. Woodson, like most authors, was proud of his *History of the Negro Church*; he asked to check all the proofs, including the captions beneath the illustrations.

When the first fifty copies of his new book reached him, Woodson angrily exploded. The printer had ignored Woodson's request about checking all proofs before the book was printed. "Now you have done the very thing that I thought you might do," Woodson declared. "The second illustration in the book, 'The Oldest Negro Baptist Church in the United States,' carries at the bottom of it the inscription 'Uncle Tom's Cabin,' a thing that I never dreamed of."[11] The printer had no choice but to take back the fifty copies, correct the error, and reissue the book.

Woodson also published his first textbook in 1922, *The Negro in Our History*. Books about African Americans and their part in United States history were still in short supply. Woodson's textbook filled a great need. It helped black schools, especially in the South, introduce courses in African-American history. The first edition of the textbook sold out in less than a year. The second edition, in 1923, also sold quickly. With the help of a research assistant, Woodson expanded and updated the third edition of the textbook.

While Woodson's popular textbook clearly met a need, it also had some drawbacks. It was not smoothly written, for one thing. Also, Woodson made too many sweeping statements that were not supported by evidence. By the time the ninth edition of Woodson's textbook appeared in 1947, another historian had written a better, more comprehensive, and more balanced textbook. John Hope Franklin, a much younger African-American historian than Woodson, first published *From Slavery to Freedom: A History of Negro Americans* in 1947. It was destined to go through many editions. It became a classic text and reference book, and it is still going strong today.

Woodson's textbook, in short, did not live as long as some of his other contributions did. He had more ideas for topics in black history than he could cover by himself. He wanted to assign some of these topics to younger historians. He would help train them to do research and to write up the results. All of that required money.

Again Woodson turned to rich foundations in New York to ask for money for the research program. One or two foundations turned him down, but Woodson kept trying. The Laura Spelman Rockefeller Memorial Fund was one of several philanthropic organizations of the oil-rich Rockefeller family. In 1922, it gave Woodson another $25,000. This money was also to be paid in $5,000 installments over a five-year period. All of it was to be used for Woodson's research program; none could be used to pay the expenses of the association or the *Journal of Negro History*.

The first young African-American scholar whom Woodson hired was A. A. Taylor. He was also someone who managed to get along with Woodson over a period of several years. A native of Washington, D.C., Taylor had taught history at West Virginia Collegiate Institute while Woodson also taught there. Woodson encouraged Taylor to seek advanced training at Harvard, and he helped pay the bills as the younger man worked for his master's degree and then his Ph.D. Taylor had begun doing research on the Reconstruction period even before he went to Harvard. His Ph.D. dissertation was titled, "The Negro in South Carolina During the Reconstruction." After that Taylor did a

Alrutheus Ambush (A. A.) Taylor was the first young African-American scholar to join Woodson's research staff. Taylor went on to become a well-known historian.

similar study of Virginia. Woodson helped with these projects. He also published both of them in the *Journal of Negro History* and in separate books issued by Associated Publishers.[12]

Taylor was not the only young African-American scholar helped by Woodson. Most of them were men, but Woodson was also happy to work with women scholars. One of them, who later became famous as a novelist, was Zora Neale Hurston. While she was a graduate student at Columbia University, Hurston collected black folktales for Woodson and interviewed former slaves still living in her native Florida and in nearby Alabama.[13]

Two young African-American scholars whom Woodson hired as research assistants were Lorenzo J. Greene and Charles H. Wesley. Both later became well-known historians. Another younger historian who helped Woodson on a number of projects was Rayford W. Logan. Woodson grew unhappy with both Wesley and Logan and their work. Consequently, he fired them—as he did many who associated themselves with him.

Despite his prickly personality, Woodson continued to be full of first-rate ideas. In 1926, he started the annual celebration of Negro History Week. Woodson had earlier worked for several years with an African-American fraternity at Fisk University in Nashville, Tennessee. At Woodson's urging, the fraternity in 1920 had begun sponsoring a weeklong celebration of African-American history and literature. When the fraternity stopped doing this in 1925, Woodson saw an opportunity for the Association for the Study of Negro Life and History. The organization became the sponsor for a nationwide observance of what Woodson named Negro History Week.

Woodson picked the second week of February for the celebration. He chose that time because both Frederick Douglass, the most famous African-American leader of the Civil War era, and Abraham Lincoln were born in that month.

Woodson prepared a brief pamphlet for the first Negro History Week. He wrote a short history of the Association for the Study of Negro Life and History. He also listed subjects that could be studied and discussed, with a list of recommended books. Various outstanding African Americans, both living and dead, received special notice.

In later years Woodson put together more-elaborate Negro History Week Kits. He included pictures of outstanding blacks and special stories for children about African-American leaders in various fields of activity. For adults, Woodson prepared study guides.

With Negro History Week, Woodson was trying to reach a larger audience. After all, as valuable as the *Journal of Negro History* was, it reached mainly scholars. Woodson mailed his Negro History Week Kits to preachers, teachers, club presidents, publishers of black newspapers, and anyone else who he thought would help promote black history.

By 1929, Woodson's association was selling repro-ductions of 160 photographs of important African Americans. There were also specialized pamphlets that included lists of books and articles on various topics in black history. Woodson prepared the "Table of 152 Important Events and Dates in Negro History." By the early 1930s, this publication sold for fifty cents.

Negro History Week grew to include many different activities. In the larger cities there were parades with people in costumes portraying famous blacks. Breakfasts, banquets, poetry readings, exhibits, talks about some particular aspect of African-American history—all these and more became part of the event.

In 1930, Woodson arranged for a Negro History Week program that proved especially successful. During the Reconstruction Era and for some years after, a number of southern blacks were elected to the United States House of Representatives. By 1930, with southern blacks stripped of the right to vote, there were no African-American congressmen from the South. There was, however, the first African-American member of Congress elected from the North, Oscar DePriest of Chicago, Illinois.

Some of the former congressmen from the South were still living in 1930. Woodson arranged to have them and DePriest speak at a large banquet meeting. More than two thousand people attended, and Woodson raised some money for additional materials for Negro History Week.[14]

By the 1940s, the celebrations of Negro History Week had grown more elaborate and more numerous across the nation. Lectures were sponsored by organizations for African-American women and by social service groups. Schools, libraries, and museums put up exhibits. Teachers attended special institutes or classes to prepare for the event, and they assigned essays on topics in black history in their classes.

Woodson gave much of the credit for the success of Negro History Week to the schoolteachers. He wrote regularly in the *Journal of Negro History* and in African-American newspapers about the most creative programs in various schools. In 1935, he reported that Texas, Georgia, and Delaware had put black history in the course of study for both the junior and senior high schools. Alabama and South Carolina were about to do the same thing.

In the cities of the North first, and then much later in the South, white politicians got into the act. Mayors and governors began issuing official statements in honor of Negro History Week. Woodson had the satisfaction of seeing the celebration of Negro History Week spread into some Latin American countries, the West Indies, and Africa.[15]

Looking back later, the historian Rayford Logan declared that Negro History Week was "the best work" of promotion that had been done for African Americans. He believed that "literally tens of thousands of people have come to have a higher appreciation of the Negro. . . . If Negro History Week has done nothing else, it has removed this inferiority complex from the thinking of large numbers of Negroes and has given many others a sense of pride and optimism."[16]

W. E. B. Du Bois was not a close friend of Woodson's. Yet Du Bois hailed Negro History Week as Woodson's "crowning achievement." According to Du Bois, Woodson had "literally made this country, which has only the slightest respect for people of color, recognize and celebrate each year . . . the effect the American Negro has had upon the life, thought and action in the United States." Du Bois concluded with this tribute to Woodson: "I know of no one man who in a lifetime has, unaided, built up such a national celebration."[17]

There was a fairly small group of racially liberal whites who showed an interest in Negro History Week from the start. It was not until after the civil rights movement of the 1950s and 1960s, however, that large numbers of whites began to be interested in the event. In time, the entire month of February, not just a week, became dedicated to a nationwide observance of African-American history.

During 1926, the same year that Woodson began Negro History Week, he received the NAACP's Spingarn Medal. It was given every year to an African American who had excelled in his or her field of activity.[18]

The honor and recognition probably meant a great deal to Woodson. Working as hard as he always did, he still lived a lonely bachelor's life. He did not take the award of the Spingarn Medal as a signal to ease up. He still had much more to accomplish in the service of African-American history.

7

AT THE PEAK OF HIS CAREER

y the time Woodson received the NAACP's Spingarn Medal in 1926, his own scholarly achievements were impressive. He had written or compiled six books. He had authored eight carefully footnoted articles for the *Journal of Negro History* and reviewed more than ninety books in the same journal. He had also collected and published in the journal a rich assortment of documents relating to black history. All of these achievements were in addition to his having established the Association for the Study of Negro Life and History, the *Journal of*

Negro History, Associated Publishers, and Negro History Week. Woodson's citation for the Spingarn Medal simply said, "For ten years' service in collecting and publishing records of the Negro in America. . . . "[1]

Amid all of Woodson's varied activities, he spent a great deal of time traveling around the country giving talks about the association and its work. He spoke to the congregations of African-American churches, to interracial reform organizations sponsored by religious groups, to teachers' associations, and to the faculty and students of African-American colleges. There were also black fraternal and cultural groups that were glad to hear Woodson speak.

Aside from promoting the study of African-American history, Woodson had to keep trying to raise money. The 1922 grant that he had received from the Laura Spelman Rockefeller Memorial Fund in support of his research and publication program had been for a five-year period. As the fifth year approached, Woodson hoped to persuade the foundation to renew and even increase its support. Thinking big, Woodson asked for three times as much money as his original grant; this time he requested $15,000 a year for five years. Prominent white scholars, at Woodson's request, wrote letters supporting his proposal. One of them noted, "It is rather difficult to cooperate with him, but his work is credible."[2]

Woodson did not get as much money as he asked

for from the Laura Spelman Rockefeller Memorial Fund. Yet he still did better than he had done before. The foundation agreed to provide $7,600 a year for research and $5,000 a year for publication for a three-year period.

Still, Woodson's luck with the rich foundations was beginning to run out. The foundation officials continued to worry about the fact that Woodson tended to run a one-man show. He still refused to associate the *Journal of Negro History* with an African-American college or university. If Woodson became ill or died, what would happen to the journal and the other activities that he had started? Woodson proved immovable. He argued that "none of the so-called Negro universities has carried out a research program or produced through their professors any work appraised as scientifically valuable." He conceded that someday the situation might change so that it would be possible to link the journal with an African-American college or university. For the time being, though, he insisted that "there is such little interest in the work [of black history] at any one institution" that it could "be better taken care of through one national organization" than put someplace "where few persons have developed sufficiently to understand what it means."[3]

Woodson may or may not have been unfair in expressing such a low opinion of the work in African-American history then being done at African-American schools. What he seemed to forget was that if the work then being done was not up to the desired standard, then he could certainly pitch in and help improve the situation. The truth was that Woodson had grown accustomed to doing things his own way and being his own boss. He sadly lacked the ability to work with—and especially under—other people. He would eventually pay a price for his go-it-alone policy.

The Rockefeller Foundation officers were clearly annoyed by Woodson's stubbornness, but they still stood by him and his work. In 1929, they awarded him $10,000 for one year only. They also explained that any renewal of the grant would depend upon Woodson's ability to get additional financial support from other sources. Standing by their own beliefs, they also again urged Woodson to associate the journal with one of the African-American colleges.

Disappointed that the Rockefeller Foundation had not given him as much help as requested, Woodson turned to the Rosenwald Fund. He asked for $81,000 to start more than a half dozen new research projects. Although Julius Rosenwald himself continued to support Woodson's work, the Rosenwald Fund, which had its own director and board, refused to grant Woodson the money.[4]

The Rockefeller Foundation continued to be Woodson's best hope. In 1930, after the one-year grant had been spent, Rockefeller again supported Woodson, this time giving a three-year matching grant totaling $22,500. This meant that each year for three years, Woodson would have to raise $7,500 from other sources in order to receive $7,500 from the Rockefeller Foundation. Raising the $7,500 matching money was a difficult job. Over the three-year period, white individuals and foundations gave Woodson the largest single sums of money, whereas blacks made smaller contributions. According to one of Woodson's biographers, he had to donate part of his own salary in order to match the Rockefeller grant. It was a struggle, but he managed to do it.[5]

Woodson was finally at the end of his rope with the foundations. When he tried to get the Rockefeller grant renewed in 1933, he failed. This time the foundation officers insisted that Woodson would have to associate the *Journal of Negro History* as well as his research program with an African-American educational institution. John Hope, the distinguished president of Atlanta University, tried to persuade Woodson to let the university provide office space and financial support for the journal. Hope had made the offer twice before. Woodson turned it down—again.[6]

Despite Woodson's repeated requests, both the Rockefeller Foundation and the Rosenwald Fund refused further help. After 1933, in fact, no white foundation gave much money to the association or to the journal. Woodson was forced to turn, as one of his

John Hope, president of Atlanta University, wanted Woodson to associate the *Journal of Negro History* with his university, but Woodson preferred to remain independent.

biographers explains, "from whites to his own people." He "began to solicit the nickel-and-dime support that kept the organization in operation throughout the rest of his life."[7]

Frustrated, Woodson became bitter toward both the foundations and certain prominent whites who had earlier supported him and his work. He now conveniently overlooked the fact that the foundations had given him important support for more than ten years. Some of Woodson's angry statements in the 1930s led W. E. B. Du Bois to say that Woodson had developed a "deep-seated dislike, if not hatred, for the white people."[8]

Woodson's money worries after 1933 were a result of his own stubborn policies. He strongly preferred to run a one-man show, and he was finding that there was a painful price to pay for that. Fortunately, he did not let money problems keep him from coming up with first-rate ideas. He had to scale back, but his work kept going.

By 1937, Negro History Week had grown so popular that more material was needed at all levels in the public schools. There was also a need for a publication that reached beyond the limited audience of the *Journal of Negro History*. To fill the gap, Woodson began publishing the *Negro History Bulletin* in 1937. It appeared nine times a year while schools were in session.

With many photographs of current and past African-American leaders, the bulletin also carried biographical information on them. Woodson wanted to make the publication attractive to a large audience. He often organized a single issue around a central theme such as the antislavery movement or blacks in art, literature, science, education, religion, and business. Some issues focused on blacks in other parts of the world.

The *Negro History Bulletin* included a children's page with news about how students and their teachers were observing Negro History Week. A column on books offered suggestions and brief reviews. Woodson frequently published stories and essays on topics in black history that were written by school-children.

In the bulletin's editorials, Woodson attacked white racism and various injustices suffered by blacks. He urged his readers to save, to stay out of debt, and, whenever possible, to buy from black-owned business-es. During World War II, many African Americans, and even some whites, became more outspoken about the plight of America's largest minority. The *Negro History Bulletin* both reflected and stimulated that rising protest. Woodson even argued around 1945 that the new United Nations organization should not allow the United States to join until it had corrected its own racial problems.[9]

The foundations had ended their help. The bulletin helped Woodson to make up at least a part of the support for his work that he had lost. Other people helped him raise money, too. In the late 1930s, Charles Wesley, a well-known historian at Howard University, and Susie Quander, a schoolteacher in Washington, D.C., helped out. They led the Nationwide One-Dollar Sustaining Membership Drive. Twenty-seven state chairpersons assisted. Wesley, who had picked up Woodson's view, argued: "A thousand Negroes who will give one dollar to the cause are in the long run of more real value to the Association than many times a thousand dollars from a foundation which desires to direct its publication[s] and influence its thinking."[10]

The Association for the Study of Negro Life and History was twenty-five years old in 1940. Woodson asked African Americans who were able to do so to contribute $25 to the "Silver Anniversary Fund." In this way he raised $7,000.

Another African-American historian who significantly aided Woodson was Luther Porter Jackson of Virginia State College. On Woodson's behalf, Jackson wrote countless letters, gave many lectures, and made appeals to all sorts of African-American organizations in Virginia. Woodson expressed his gratitude for the help. He said that Jackson was "one among ten thousand, for history shows that only this small proportion

Charles H. Wesley worked with Woodson on a number of projects and became a prominent historian at Howard University.

of the human race is interested in preserving and publishing its record to generations unborn."[11]

The *Negro History Bulletin* helped increase the membership of the association. During Woodson's lifetime, its annual meetings, which were always biracial, had to be held in black-owned facilities. This was because the major hotels, in the North as well as in the South, were not open to African Americans.

The association's programs were also a bit different from those of other historical groups. As would be expected, there were sessions on various topics in black history, where scholars read papers or prominent leaders gave talks. Before or after each session, however, a local singer or a church choir would perform. "This was very much in keeping with the tradition within the Negro society of the time," according to one of Woodson's biographers.[12]

In later years the association met frequently on the campuses of African-American colleges or universities. Even then, an evening session, and usually the opening one, was held in a local African-American church. Not until 1964, fourteen years after Woodson's death, did the association hold its annual meeting in a major hotel.

Woodson and his co-workers carefully designed programs to appeal to both scholarly and general audiences. Instead of having only historians on the program committee, the Association for the Study of

Negro Life and History also included public-school teachers, businesspeople, club women, and ministers. As a result, amateur historians as well as professionally trained ones read papers, and different programs were designed for different groups.

Woodson also used the annual meetings of the association to display the richness of the African-American cultural heritage. He invited black poets, musicians, painters, sculptors, and other artists to appear on the programs and display their talents. In a large meeting in New York in 1931, for example, a musical program and a lecture on black music followed a festive dinner. The Harlem branch of the New York Public Library put up a special exhibit on black literature and art.

In Washington, D.C., at the 1933 meeting, in addition to musical programs and art exhibits, prominent African-American poets, including Countee Cullen and Langston Hughes, read from their work. During the 1945 meeting in Columbus, Ohio, the attending members visited several museums and libraries to see exhibits about the role of blacks in Ohio's history.[13]

Despite all the variety in the programs, Woodson always kept a major emphasis on his favorite subject: the teaching of African-American history. Not only did teachers discuss the methods and materials that had worked best for them, but parents, ministers, and club women also dealt with the subject.

One of Woodson's younger associates later explained that for Carter G. Woodson, black history was an instrument, a tool, "to help black people achieve equality of citizenship in American society." It was, Woodson believed, the essential thing needed to enable African Americans "to be respected and to respect themselves."[14]

8

LAST YEARS AND LEGACY

oodson expected the younger historians who sometimes worked with him to put in long hours. But he always worked longer, and harder, than anybody around him. His chief activities involved research, writing, editing, and organizing—all made use of his well-developed professional skills. Yet he was not above certain lowly tasks.

One of the younger black scholars whom Woodson employed in the late 1920s, Lorenzo J. Greene, later noted that Woodson usually worked sixteen to eighteen hours a day. Woodson explained to Greene that work in the coal mines of West Virginia as a young man had made him strong. Woodson said that his long hours did not bother him.

In addition to his regular, professional work, Woodson cooked his own meals and did all sorts of cleaning in the headquarters building where he worked and lived. Greene reported that on many mornings he would arrive early at the office and find Woodson, shabbily dressed, busily cleaning the office.

One day Greene entered his office and found Woodson oiling the floor. Greene offered to do the job himself. "Mr. Greene," Woodson gruffly replied, "I did not hire you to be a janitor."[1]

Despite his hard work, Woodson did something in 1933, and in several following years, that he had not done before: He took a vacation. It was partly a working vacation, but it was in a choice spot—Paris, France.

Woodson had greatly enjoyed and profited from his visit to Paris back in 1907. Now, as a much older man of fifty-eight, he returned to the beautiful City of Light. The cost of living in Paris, as in the rest of Europe, was quite low in the 1930s. The U.S. dollar would pay for or buy a great deal, so living in Paris then was nothing like the shock to the pocketbook that it would be now.

Paris held many attractions for Woodson. He visited the numerous rare-book shops and reported that in 1933 alone he bought more than three hundred out-of-print books. They dealt with the slave trade and

Lorenzo J. Greene was another of the many young African-American historians employed by Carter Woodson. Later, Greene wrote about the years he spent studying African-American history at Woodson's side.

slavery in colonial America, Haiti, and the British West Indies, among other topics. Some of the books were important enough for Woodson to hope that his Associated Publishers could reprint them—if the necessary funds were available.

He returned to the National Library of France, one of the world's richest collections, and searched for documents relating to African as well as African-American history. Woodson consulted with French researchers and scholars. He was so impressed by two of the French scholars that he later helped to bring them to the United States to give lectures.[2]

Even as he enjoyed some of the fine food for which France is famous, Woodson continued to work. Among Woodson's papers in the Library of Congress are some menus saved from Parisian restaurants where he dined. On one menu, Woodson filled both sides with research notes; on another, he made notes for a review of a book on slavery that he was reading. As one of his biographers suggests, "Here was a lonely man, in beautiful Paris, eating fine food, and yet never far away from the cause [and work] to which he was devoted."[3]

Woodson was not, however, always alone in Paris. On another visit, in 1935, he ran into an African-American couple he knew from home, and he invited them to be his guests at dinner. This was a side of Woodson that few people knew. The man Woodson had befriended commented later that it had been "a great pleasure" to learn in Paris that Woodson did not always scorn some of life's small treats. Woodson, the man had discovered, was "a 'regular fellow' as well as a distinguished scholar."[4]

When World War II began in Europe in 1939, Woodson's summer visits to Paris ended. He continued to exchange letters with French scholars who shared his interest in African history.

Although the end of foundation support forced a cutback, Woodson's Associated Publishers continued to publish scholarly books by blacks in the 1930s and 1940s. With Woodson himself doing the editing, more than a dozen books were published. By the late 1930s, funds were so scarce that Woodson had to ask the authors to pay for the costs of publishing their books. Woodson also asked African-American organizations to help with publication costs. There were African-American fraternities and sororities that each gave $100 a year for the purpose.[5]

Woodson had long been interested in Africa and its history. As a result, in 1936 he wrote and published *The African Background Outlined* and in 1939 another book, *African Heroes and Heroines*. Woodson hoped that his work in African history would, as he explained, "invite attention to the vastness of Africa and the complex problems of conflicting cultures." He was interested not only in the native peoples of the African continent but also in the more important European whites "who have vitally affected their lives and shaped the destiny of Africa."[6] At one point Woodson hoped to publish a large *Encyclopedia Africana*, but unfortunately he did not get that done.

Woodson did not allow his interest in African history to keep him from writing about matters closer to home. In 1933, his book *The Mis-Education of the Negro* attacked what he saw as glaring failures in the schooling being offered to African Americans. Stepping on toes right and left, Woodson claimed that African-American colleges and universities were failing to teach their students about their own history. Moreover, he accused the schools of not even teaching their students how to make a living.

Woodson said that "if by the teaching of history the white man could be further assured of his superiority and the Negro could be made to feel that he had always been a failure . . . ," then "the freedman would still be a slave."[7] Woodson deeply believed that knowledge of black history was essential for the mental and psychological health of African Americans. Consequently, he lashed out at more prosperous African Americans—middle-class lawyers, doctors, teachers, businesspeople, and others—whom he accused of neglecting black history. They also, Woodson argued, were unconcerned about the mass of poor African Americans in urban ghettoes and on southern farms.

In presenting his arguments about education, Woodson expressed his views that resembled those of both Booker T. Washington and W. E. B. Du Bois. Woodson praised Washington as a brilliant educator who had "revolutionized" the schooling of African Americans. Yet Woodson also supported Du Bois's idea about the need for a "talented tenth" among the race. After all, both Du Bois and Woodson were living examples of what such highly educated African Americans could do. Woodson went on to insist that too many members of the educated, African-American middle class had become too distanced from the mass of black people. "The majority of this [middle] class," Woodson declared, "go through life denouncing white people because they are trying to run away from blacks and decrying the blacks because they are not white."[8]

Like many other historians of his time, both white and black, Woodson never announced his loyalty to either of the nation's major political parties. That is, he refused to label himself either a Republican or a Democrat. He had argued during World War I, for example, that blacks "should support representative men of any color or party, if they stand for a square deal and equal rights for all." Blacks, he believed, should vote for "those men who are fair-minded and considerate of the man far down, and seek to embrace their many opportunities for economic progress, a foundation for political recognition, upon which the race must learn to build."[9]

Historically, the great majority of black men who gained the vote after the Civil War had become loyal Republicans. That party, led by Abraham Lincoln, had succeeded in winning the Civil War and destroying slavery. White Democrats in the South had managed to rob southern blacks of the right to vote in the years just before and after 1900. But in the North, African Americans remained mostly Republican.

Woodson lived to observe several significant changes affecting the lives of African Americans. The outbreak of World War I in Europe in 1914 halted much of the flood of immigrants that had been pouring into the cities of the northeastern United States and providing cheap labor in industries and businesses. This stoppage, plus the economic boom that had developed by the time the United States entered the war in 1917, created labor shortages in the North.

Lured by jobs and the hope of a better life, African Americans began a great migration out of the South around 1916. They poured into the cities of the North and the West. In 1918, Woodson wrote a short book about this subject: *A Century of Negro Migration*. He proved to be quite correct when he wrote that "this new [migration] phase of Negro American life . . . will doubtless prove to be the most significant event" in African-American history since the Civil War. Woodson optimistically believed in 1918 that the whole nation would be "benefitted by this upheaval" in where blacks lived. In the South, especially in those areas where blacks outnumbered whites, he believed that the great migration would, as he put it, "remove the fear of *Negro domination*, one of the causes of the backwardness of the South and its peculiar civilization."[10]

As rural southern blacks poured into northern cities, Woodson was also keenly aware that there would be friction and problems. He again proved to be correct, for in 1919 fierce race riots broke out in a number of cities across the land.[11]

The economic depression that hit the country after 1929 slowed the tide of African Americans moving to the North. The Great Depression also inspired the Democrats and their popular president, Franklin D. Roosevelt, to start the New Deal and its program of reforms. By the time Roosevelt ran for his second term in 1936, a great change in African-American voting had taken place: Leaving the party of Lincoln, most African Americans who could vote chose to vote for Roosevelt. For the remainder of Woodson's life, and long after, that would remain true. Yet Woodson stood pat on his own policy of not committing himself to either party.[12]

Woodson liked to think for himself, and he also refused to bow before popular styles and trends. Even in his lifetime, there was debate about the preferred name for the black race. When Woodson was growing up in the late nineteenth century, many blacks and well-meaning whites used the term *colored* to refer to blacks. The word *black* was then considered a bit harsh—but not as harsh as the term *nigger*, which was a nasty insult when used by whites. The word *negro* was also widely used, even in the 1800s, but it was not generally capitalized. Many black leaders, such as W. E. B. Du Bois, insisted that the word *Negro* should be spelled with a capital *N*. This idea gradually caught on among educated people of both races. In 1930, *The New York Times*, perhaps the leading newspaper in the nation, explained in an editorial that from that time on it would use a capital *N* for the word *Negro*. The *Times* declared: "It is an act of recognition of racial self-respect for those who have been for generations in 'the lower case.' "[13]

Someone asked Woodson at a professional meeting of historians about the correct name for the race. With his characteristic straight talk, he replied: "It does not matter so much what the thing is called as what the thing is. The Negro would not cease to be what he is by calling him something else. . . ." He added that there was "nothing to be gained by running away from the name."[14]

Woodson did not live to see the triumphant civil rights movement of the 1950s and 1960s. If he had, he would have welcomed the proud use of the term *black* which largely replaced *Negro* in the 1960s. And then, even later, the more fully descriptive and accurate term *African American* came into widespread use. In fact, in 1970 Woodson's successors changed the name of the association that he had established to the Association for the Study of Afro-American Life and History.

Carter G. Woodson, age seventy-four, died during the night of April 3, 1950. He was alone at his office-home in Washington, D.C.

From the 1960s onward, the understanding of the role of African Americans in the nation's past moved steadily closer to the ideas that Woodson had championed throughout his life. Beginning in the 1950s, historians, both black and white, stopped looking at slavery through rose-colored glasses and began to reveal the truth. Ideas about slavery that Woodson and some other black historians had pushed much earlier—only to be ignored by most white historians—became accepted and standard across the nation.

After hearing stories directly from his own father as well as from other African-American veterans of the Union army, Woodson knew that African Americans had played an important role in the North's victory in the Civil War. Yet white Americans either forgot or ignored that fact for many decades after the war. Through articles in the *Journal of Negro History* and

This postage stamp was released in recognition of the valuable contributions made by Carter G. Woodson to the field of African-American history.

some of his own writings, Woodson tried to get the truth told. Then finally, beginning in the 1960s—some years after Woodson died—his version became the mainstream version.

The same thing happened concerning the black role in Reconstruction. Woodson and several of the younger historians whom he helped train—A. A. Taylor, Charles Wesley, Lorenzo Greene, and others— tried to make known a truer, fairer understanding of the African-American role in Reconstruction. They, and W. E. B. Du Bois, largely failed in that effort during the 1920s and 1930s. Later the tide changed, especially from the 1960s onward. The views that the pioneer African-American historians had advanced became the mainstream views.

Black college students and their white allies had to fight for the cause of black history in the 1960s. They won. Woodson would have had every reason to be proud as African-American history became a well-established and respected field of study across the nation from the late 1960s onward.

Woodson earned a reputation among many who knew him as a gruff, quarrelsome man. Yet there were always those who knew that he actually hid or masked certain kinder, more caring qualities. The African-American historian John Hope Franklin, who was younger than Woodson, got help and advice from him. Franklin later remembered Woodson as "one of the most charming men I ever met." Franklin declared that he never saw in Woodson "any of the peculiarities or unfavorable side of his personality that others claimed he possessed." Woodson, Franklin concluded, was just "so desperately anxious that the history of the Negro would be integrated into the history of the United States."[15]

Benjamin Quarles, another black historian who was younger than Woodson, recalled that Woodson was "quick to smile or laugh" and "had a ready sense of humor." He was direct and straightforward in what he said, "making him seem a bit blunt." Quarles went on to say that in the "upsurge of black studies" that began in the late 1960s, there was "no figure to whom there is and will continue to be a greater indebtedness than to Woodson, [and] his sun is now brighter than ever before."[16]

The rich foundation officers who feared that Woodson's work might die with him proved to be wrong. The Association for the Study of Afro-American Life and History continued in full vigor after Woodson's death. The *Journal of Negro History*, later linked to Morehouse College, continued to be one of the leading scholarly journals in its field. Each February, Black History Month is observed throughout the nation.

Carter Godwin Woodson, the son of former slaves in Virginia, scrambled long and hard for an education.

The distinguished historian John Hope Franklin came to know Woodson in his later, perhaps more mellow, years. Franklin found Woodson to be "one of the most charming men" he had ever met.

He finally attained a Ph.D. in history from Harvard University. He is the only person with once-enslaved parents to earn such a distinction. He devoted most of his adult life to the cause of African-American history and left a rich legacy for all those, both black and white, who came after him.

CHRONOLOGY

1875—Carter Godwin Woodson is born on a farm near the James River in rural Virginia.

1892—Goes to West Virginia to work on the railroads and in the coal mines.

1895—Enters high school in Huntington, West Virginia.

1897—Graduates from high school and enters Berea College in Kentucky.

1898—Lack of money forces Woodson to drop out of Berea and teach school in West Virginia.

1901—Returns to Berea on part-time basis.

1903—Graduates from Berea; goes to the Philippine Islands to teach English and other subjects to Filipino youth.

1906—Returns to United States.

1907—Travels in Asia, Europe, and northern Africa; enrolls at the University of Chicago.

1908—Receives another undergraduate degree and then a master's degree in history from the University of Chicago; enters Harvard University.

1909—Leaves Harvard after one year because of lack of money; begins teaching in the public schools of Washington, D.C.

1910—Passes general examination for advanced degree in history at Harvard.

1912—Receives Ph.D. in history from Harvard.

1915—Publishes his first book, *The Education of the Negro Prior to 1861*; takes lead in starting the Association for the Study of Negro Life and History; begins editing and publishing the *Journal of Negro History.*

1919—Resigns as a school principal in Washington, D.C., to accept appointment at Howard University; introduces African-American history courses there.

1920—Disagrees publicly with president of Howard and is fired by the trustees; becomes dean of the college department at West Virginia Collegiate Institute.

1921—Establishes Associated Publishers in Washington, D.C.; publishes *The History of the Negro Church.*

1922—Resigns from West Virginia Collegiate Institute; becomes full-time, paid director of research and editor of *Journal of Negro History*; buys a house in Washington, D.C., to serve as headquarters of the Association for the Study of Negro Life and History and lives on the top floor; publishes his widely used textbook, *The Negro in Our History.*

1926—Launches annual celebration in February of Negro History Week; receives the Spingarn Medal from the National Association for the Advancement of Colored People.

1928—Places valuable collection of documents relating to African-American history in the Library of Congress.

1933—Publishes *The Mis-Education of the Negro*.

1936—Publishes *The African Background Outlined*.

1937—Begins publishing the *Negro History Bulletin*.

1939—Publishes *African Heroes and Heroines*.

1950—Dies on April 3 at age seventy-four in his office-home in Washington, D.C.

CHAPTER NOTES

Chapter 1. A Well-Deserved Honor
1. John H. Holmes, "On Presenting the Spingarn Medal," *Crisis*, vol. 32 (September 1926), p. 233.
2. Holmes, p. 234.
3. Jacqueline Goggin, *Carter G. Woodson: A Life in Black History* (Baton Rouge: Louisiana State University Press, 1993), p. 9.

Chapter 2. In the Shadow of Slavery
1. Jacqueline Goggin, *Carter G. Woodson: A Life in Black History* (Baton Rouge: Louisiana State University Press, 1993), pp. 1–2.
2. Goggin, pp. 2–3.
3. Carter G. Woodson, "My Recollections of Veterans of the Civil War," *Negro History Bulletin*, vol. 7 (February 1944), p. 103.
4. Woodson, pp. 104–105.
5. Woodson, p. 104.
6. Baltimore *Afro-American*, June 25, 1932, p. 15.
7. Goggin, p. 10.
8. Woodson, pp. 115–116.
9. Woodson, p. 116.
10. Woodson, p. 117.
11. Woodson, pp. 117–118.
12. Ibid.

Chapter 3. Student, Teacher, Traveler
1. John Hope Franklin, *From Slavery to Freedom: A History of Negro Americans*, 5th ed. (New York: Knopf, 1980), pp. 263–267, 313–317.
2. Paul David Nelson, "Experiment in Interracial Education at Berea College, 1858–1908," *Journal of Negro History*, vol. 59 (1974), pp. 13–27.

3. Jacqueline Goggin, *Carter G. Woodson: A Life in Black History* (Baton Rouge: Louisiana State University Press, 1993), pp. 15–18.

4. Patricia W. Romero, "Carter G. Woodson: A Biography" (Ph.D. dissertation, Ohio State University, 1971), pp. 50–57.

Chapter 4. Making History With a Ph.D.

1. Patricia W. Romero, "Carter G. Woodson: A Biography" (Ph.D. dissertation, Ohio State University, 1971), pp. 28–29.

2. Jacqueline Goggin, *Carter G. Woodson: A Life in Black History* (Baton Rouge: Louisiana State University Press, 1993), p. 19.

3. Goggin, pp. 21–22.

4. Goggin, p. 22.

5. Romero, p. 71

6. W. Montague Cobb, "Carter G. Woodson: The Father of Negro History," *Journal of the National Medical Association*, vol. 62 (September 1970), 385–392, 402.

Chapter 5. A Mission to Educate Others

1. W. E. Woodward, as quoted in James M. McPherson, *The Negro's Civil War* (Urbana: University of Illinois Press, 1982), p. viii.

2. Thomas Dixon's role in the making of *The Birth of a Nation* is described in Raymond A. Cook, *Fire from the Flint: The Amazing Career of Thomas Dixon* (Winston-Salem: John F. Blair, 1968), pp. 161–183.

3. Jacqueline Goggin, *Carter G. Woodson: A Life in Black History* (Baton Rouge: Louisiana State University Press, 1993), p. 32.

4. For the origin of the National Association for the Advancement of Colored People and the National Urban League, see John Hope Franklin, *From Slavery to Freedom: A History of Negro Americans* (New York: Knopf, 1980), pp. 318–322.

5. Patricia W. Romero, "Carter G. Woodson: A Biography" (Ph.D. dissertation, Ohio State University, 1971), p. 94.

6. Romero, p. 162.

7. Romero, pp. 100–101.

8. Romero, pp. 103–104.

9. Goggin, p. 40.

Chapter 6. Launching Negro History Week

1. John Hope Franklin, *From Slavery to Freedom: A History of Negro Americans* (New York: Knopf, 1980), p. 407, discusses early graduate study at Howard and a few other African-American universities.

2. Jacqueline Goggin, *Carter G. Woodson: A Life in Black History* (Baton Rouge: Louisiana State University Press, 1993), p. 48.

3. Goggin, p. 49.

4. Goggin, p. 51.

5. Patricia W. Romero, "Carter G. Woodson: A Biography" (Ph.D. dissertation, Ohio State University, 1971), p. 79.

6. Ibid., pp. 129–130.

7. Ibid., pp. 121–122.

8. Goggin, p. 66.

9. Romero, p. 136.

10. Ibid., p. 138.

11. Ibid., pp. 133–134.

12. Goggin, p. 68.

13. For Hurston, see Zora Neale Hurston, *Dust Tracks on the Road: An Autobiography* (Urbana: University of Illinois Press, 1970).

14. Goggin, pp. 84–85.

15. Ibid., pp. 119–120.

16. Romero, p. 151.

17. Ibid., pp. 151–152.

18. John H. Holmes, "On Presenting the Spingarn Medal," *Crisis*, vol. 32 (September 1926), p. 233.

Chapter 7. At the Peak of His Career

1. Patricia W. Romero, "Carter G. Woodson: A Biography" (Ph.D. dissertation, Ohio State University, 1971), p. 158.
2. Jacqueline Goggin, *Carter G. Woodson: A Life in Black History* (Baton Rouge: Louisiana State University Press, 1993), p. 87.
3. Ibid., p. 90.
4. Edwin R. Embree and Julia Waxman, *Investment in People: The Story of the Julius Rosenwald Fund* (New York: Harper), 1949.
5. Goggin, pp. 90–92.
6. For John Hope, see Ridgeley Torrence, *The Story of John Hope* (New York: Macmillan, 1948).
7. Romero, pp. 181–182.
8. Ibid., p. 183.
9. Goggin, pp. 114–115.
10. Ibid., p. 116.
11. Ibid.
12. Romero, p. 120.
13. Goggin, 118–119.
14. Romero, pp. 238–239.

Chapter 8. Last Years and Legacy

1. Patricia W. Romero, "Carter G. Woodson: A Biography" (Ph.D. dissertation, Ohio State University, 1971), pp. 189–190.
2. Jacqueline Goggin, *Carter G. Woodson: A Life in Black History* (Baton Rouge: Louisiana State University Press, 1993), p. 122.
3. Romero, pp. 195–196.
4. Ibid., pp. 194–195.
5. Goggin, pp. 125–126.
6. Ibid., p. 128.
7. Carter G. Woodson, *The Mis-Education of the Negro*, as quoted in Romero, p. 258.
8. Goggin, p. 158.

9. Ibid., p. 141.

10. Carter G. Woodson, *A Century of Negro Migration* (Washington, D.C.: Associated Publishers 1918), p. 183.

11. These riots are discussed in August Meier and Elliott Rudwick, *From Plantation to Ghetto* (New York: Hill and Wang, 1976), pp. 239–242.

12. The African-American majority's shift to the Democratic Party is discussed in John Hope Franklin, *From Slavery to Freedom: A History of Negro Americans* (New York: Knopf, 1980), pp. 386–398.

13. *The New York Times*, editorial, March 7, 1930, p. 22.

14. Romero, p. 260.

15. Ibid., p. 261.

16. Ibid., pp. 261–262.

FURTHER READING

Goggin, Jacqueline. *Carter G. Woodson: A Life in Black History*. Baton Rouge: Louisiana State University Press, 1993.

Greene, Lorenzo J. *Working with Carter G. Woodson, the Father of Black History: A Diary, 1928–1930*. Arvarh E. Strickland, ed. Baton Rouge: Louisiana State University Press, 1989.

————. *Selling Black History for Carter G. Woodson: A Diary, 1930–1933*. Arvarh E. Strickland, ed. Columbia: University of Missouri Press, 1996.

Logan, Rayford W. "Carter Godwin Woodson." In Rayford W. Logan and Michael R. Winston, eds., *Dictionary of American Negro Biography*, pp. 665–667. New York: Norton, 1982.

McKissack, Patricia, and Fredrick McKissack. *Carter G. Woodson: The Father of Black History*. Springfield, N.J.: Enslow Publishers, Inc., 1991.

Romero, Patricia W. "Carter G. Woodson: A Biography." Ph.D. dissertation, Ohio State University, 1971. Available through University Microfilms.

Scally, Sister Mary Anthony. *Carter G. Woodson: A Bio-Bibliography*. Westport, Conn.: Greenwood Press, 1985.

Woodson, Carter G. *The African Background Outlined; or, Handbook for the Study of the Negro*. New York: Greenwood Publishing Group, Inc., 1969.

————. *African Heroes and Heroines.* Associated Publishers, Inc., 1990.

————. *African Myths Together with Proverbs.* Washington: Associated Publishers, Inc., 1964.

————. *The History of the Negro Church.* Washington: Associated Publishers, Inc., 1990.

————. *The Mis-Education of the Negro.* Washington: Associated Publishers, Inc., 1990.

————. *The Negro in Our History.* Washington: Associated Publishers, Inc., 1990.

————, and Charles H. Wesley. *Negro Makers of History.* Washington: Associated Publishers, Inc., 1968.

INDEX